501 tips for teachers

501 tips for teachers

Kid-Tested Ideas, Strategies, and Inspirations

Robert D. Ramsey, Ed.D.

CB

CONTEMPORARY BOOKS

Library of Congress Cataloging-in-Publication Data

Ramsey, Robert D.
 501 tips for teachers : kid-tested ideas, strategies,
 and inspirations / Robert D. Ramsey.
  p. cm.
  ISBN 0-8092-3042-9
  1. Teaching. 2. Teachers. 3. Teacher-
 student relationships. I. Title.
 LB1025.3.R36 1997
 371.102—dc21   97-18252
                              CIP

Cover and interior design by Monica Baziuk

Published by Contemporary Books
An imprint of NTC/Contemporary Publishing Company
4255 West Touhy Avenue, Lincolnwood (Chicago), Illinois
60646-1975 U.S.A.
Printed in the United States of America
International Standard Book Number: 0-8092-3042-9

15 14 13 12 11 10 9 8 7 6 5 4 3

Contents

Introduction

George Bernard Shaw said, "Those who can, do; those who can't, teach." George was wrong! Today's teachers have to be doers. They also have to be dreamers, schemers, helpers, healers, mentors, role models, nurturers, and inspirations. Teachers are expected to be dynamite every morning and to grade papers every night. Shaw was off the mark. Teaching today isn't for wimps, wannabees, or also-rans. It's society's most important, challenging profession, and it's getting more difficult all the time.

In classrooms at all levels, problems are proliferating and expectations are escalating. Schools across the country are being called on to do more with less. Consequently, teachers everywhere are now looking for new sources of information and motivation. Fortunately, help is available. Sometimes, the cavalry comes in the form of a little book filled with big ideas.

To succeed today, teachers need bold new ideas for helping and handling kids, as well as timeless insights into the nature of successful teaching and learning. *501 Tips for Teachers* offers both. It is a sanity-saving resource for teachers of all subjects and grade levels.

This powerful collection of school-tested teaching techniques, classroom management strategies, life-tested affirmations, and everyday encouragements has been gleaned from a career-long association with successful teachers at all levels. It includes fresh ideas whose time has come, coupled with reminders of surefire, established methods that never fail.

Used as an ever-ready source of coaching and encouragement, *501 Tips for Teachers* can help make teaching easier and more fun. Let it give you the jump start you need to be a better teacher every day—starting now!

501 tips for teachers

1.

Classroom Teaching Tips

1 Be flexible. "Schedule" a little spontaneity into your lesson plans to take advantage of the "teachable moment."

2.

Set up an Energy Outlet Space in the classroom where "pumped-up" students can scribble, use a punching bag, or do whatever it takes to release anger, frustration, or emotion constructively.

3.

Use peer tutors in your classroom. When kids teach other kids, everyone wins.

4.

Fight boredom! You're competing with MTV.

5.

Teach all students a simple six-step problem-solving process:

- Identify the problem.
- Define limits.
- Clarify issues.
- Search for solutions.
- Take action.
- Evaluate results.

6.

Set routines. They work wonders. Kids thrive on structure and work better when they know what's coming.

7.

Get new students off to a positive start by providing a New Kid Kit containing a school map, class picture, daily schedule, class roster, and a free lunch coupon.

8.

Give your classroom a new look now and then. It will perk up attention and attitudes.

9.

Help your students get organized and stay organized. Organization is one of life's survival skills. Using a lesson reminder book is a good way to start.

10.

Break down gender stereotypes. Bring in women scientists and mathematicians as role models for young girls. Help your female students break the "glass ceilings" in schools.

11.

Vary activities often. You may like to listen to yourself lecture for an hour or more, but your students won't. They're used to commercials and station breaks.

12.

Build a winning classroom—one child at a time. You can teach an entire class only by focusing on individual learners.

13.

Teach goal-setting as a survival skill. Children don't know that setting goals can change their lives unless we tell them.

14.

Make room for fun in your classroom. Learning is important, but it shouldn't be deadly serious all the time. If education isn't fun, kids aren't going to want any.

15.

Try a little mood music in your classroom. It can help you create the proper atmosphere for any learning activity.

16.

No matter what the curriculum guide says, be sure to teach the five "Habits of the Mind"*:

🍎 Weighing evidence—How credible is the evidence for what we think we know?

🍎 Awareness of varying viewpoints—Whose viewpoint is this, and what other viewpoints might there be?

🍎 Seeing connections and relationships—How are things connected, and what is here that we have seen before?

🍎 Speculating on possibilities—Can we imagine alternatives?

🍎 Assessing value both socially and personally—What difference does it make and who cares?

*Developed by Central Park East Secondary School, New York City, New York.

17.

Expect students to do "real" work. Pride comes from accomplishment, not charity.

18.

Do whatever it takes to connect kids with computers. Arrange for loaners or checkout units if necessary. Every student—not just wealthy or middle-class students—needs access to technology.

19.

Encourage study groups in and out of the classroom. When kids team up on learning, ignorance doesn't have a chance.

20.

Be a booster for journal writing. Keeping a journal is a good way for students to vent feelings, express creativity, and practice writing skills at the same time.

21.

Allow pupils to dig deeply for knowledge. Today's learners need depth as well as breadth. Shallowness isn't a world-class standard. Occasional in-depth investigation will prepare students to compete in the world arena.

22.

The first three rules of good teaching are (1) praise, (2) praise, and (3) praise! But praise students only for honest effort and authentic accomplishment. Phony praise can lead to false pride and failed dreams later.

23.

Foster intergenerational learning experiences in your classroom. When all the generations learn and play together, everyone grows a little.

24.

Don't let a single textbook define your curriculum. Teach students to use a variety of materials (resource-based instruction) in order to get a well-rounded and well-grounded learning experience. Learning shouldn't be one-dimensional.

25.

Use assessment to drive instruction in your classroom. Let test results help you help students better. That's what test scores are for, not for penalizing or embarrassing students.

26.

Teach to a variety of learning styles. Kids don't all learn in the same way. The more you mix and match teaching techniques, the more likely you are to help all learners succeed.

27.

Refuse to inflate grades. Young people need honest feedback, not exaggerations. Kids can take reality. They just can't take lies from adults they trust.

28.

Don't rely solely on tests to tell you what your pupils can do. Students are more than scores. Find a variety of ways (for example, writing samples or performance on tasks or artwork) for students to demonstrate their knowledge. Artists use portfolios to represent the variety and range of their body of work. Why not compile student portfolios for the same purpose?

29.

Minimize "downtime" in the classroom. Strive to have worthwhile learning activities going on all the time. Students attend more regularly when they're afraid they'll miss out on something important.

30.

Make a big deal out of cooperative learning in your classroom. Today, kids need to learn that in school and in life many problems are best solved when people work together, rather than compete against each other.

31.

Whenever possible, make real-world assignments dealing with everyday student problems (for example, family relationships or neighborhood violence). Students need a reason to learn. Sometimes, "just because the teacher wants it" isn't good enough. (Note: Sometimes assignments can be "too real" for the community to handle. As a safeguard, clear controversial assignments with the principal in advance.)

32.

Use an interdisciplinary approach whenever you can. That's the way the real world works. Life happens all together, not in separate compartments.

33.

Teach students to use visualizing (imaging) techniques. Visualization is a form of mental rehearsal. What you can visualize, you may achieve.

34.

If a lesson isn't working, do something else—quickly! Bad lessons don't get better by themselves. Always have a backup plan in reserve.

35.

Stay up-to-date on what's hot and what's not in curriculum and instruction, such as the following:

What's Hot	What's Not
Active Learning	Lecture Only
Identifying Patterns	Rote Recitation
Open-Ended Questions	Single-Answer Questions
Situational Problems	Follow-the-Example Exercises

36.

Make all your lessons as multicultural, inclusive, and gender-fair as possible. Good teaching leaves no one out.

37.

Despite today's media infatuation with "sound bites," continue teaching solid writing skills. Even the Internet could benefit from clear, effective writing.

38.

Allow adequate "wait time" for students to respond to questions. Don't rush to fill the void if no one volunteers an answer immediately. A little silence can put subtle pressure on students to come forward with what they know.

39.

Never apologize for long or difficult assignments. They show you expect and value effort. All students should earn their education the old-fashioned way by working for it.

40.

Schedule the hardest lessons when your students are freshest. (Some schools are even considering delaying their start time to capitalize on periods of peak performance for most pupils.)

41.

Show your students how to set up their own filing system at home. It's never too early for kids to start relying on "files, not piles."

42.

Let your students grade themselves occasionally. Have them fill out a report card on themselves and review it with you. Discuss where you differ—and why!

43.

No matter what method of teaching reading your school follows, insist on including some phonics. It's the only way to assure that students have lifelong decoding skills.

44.

Periodically ask your students, "How can we do better as a class?" Discuss their suggestions as a group.

45.

Teach students to respect and protect the planet and its resources. It will take only one generation of ecology-conscious citizens to make peace with the environment.

46.

Continue to read aloud to students—
no matter how old they are.

47.

Teach basic school survival skills
such as memory aids, test-taking
techniques, note-taking skills, and
proofreading tips. These skills help
set up students for success.

48.

Celebrate successes—even little ones!
Encouragement is never wasted.

49.

Remember that more isn't always better. The teacher who talks the most or assigns the most doesn't always teach the most.

50.

Build students' vocabulary—no matter what subject you're teaching. Words are power. It's yours to give.

51.

Don't just shout out homework assignments as your students are walking out the door. Any assignment worth doing is worth explaining thoroughly with time to answer questions.

52.

Be approachable. Being seated behind a desk is not a welcoming position. Get up, get out, and mingle with "your people." It works for politicians, and it can work for you.

53.

Begin and end class on time—every time. Punctuality teaches a lesson. Besides, it's your job.

54.

Give students more practice in planning, thinking, and deciding and less practice in memorizing, copying, and repeating.

55.

Never teach a bad lesson twice.

56.

Keep a supply of pencils and paper available for student use. The more excuses you take away, the more likely students are to learn.

57.

Never use a worksheet when an open-ended question would work better.

58.

Always have good lesson plans ready for substitute teachers. The practice of throwing Christians to the lions went out of fashion a long time ago.

59.

All good stories have a "hook" to capture the reader's interest from the very beginning. Good lessons are the same way.

60.

Don't always call on the kids who hold up their hands. It lets all the others off the hook too easily.

61.

Keep your method of determining grades simple. It shouldn't take a CPA to figure out your marking system.

62.

Give your kids a break once in awhile—no weekend homework!

63.

Realize that students are always learning; even recess is part of the curriculum.

64.

Never give an assignment you don't intend to look at. It's a form of betrayal.

65.

Tell your classes about former students who have gone on to lead successful lives. Kids thrive on examples and role models. They need to know that achieving success can still happen.

66.

Praise students in public. Criticize them in private. Never subject a child to public humiliation. That's the number one complaint of students everywhere.

67.

Don't be a slave to your syllabus. Reaching just one student is more important than finishing a dozen textbooks.

68.

Always have more to offer. When students have mastered the lesson at hand, there should be another place for them to go intellectually.

69.

Be willing to arrive early and stay late—maybe even come in on Saturdays once in awhile—to help students who really want it and need it. If a pupil is ready to learn, a teacher should be ready to teach.

70.

Know the difference between teaching and sermonizing.

71.

Get *everyone's* attention before you start a lesson. It's worth the wait.

72.

Revisit your best lessons. Why did they work? What can work again? There's no rule against repeating success.

73.

Remember that short, direct instructions and explanations work best. There's a reason why teachers aren't paid by the word.

74.

Putting up the same old, tired displays year after year gives bulletin boards a bad name. Turn the job over to your kids. Your classroom will be a livelier, more interesting place because of it.

75.

Keep a supply of brainteasers and puzzles on hand for the kids who always finish before the rest of the class does. When students are ready for more, they should get it.

76.

Try scheduling the study period at the beginning of class, instead of at the end. The students will be fresher, and they may not waste so much time clock-watching.

77.

Be a stickler for neatness and cleanliness in the classroom. The world's messy enough. We don't need to teach tomorrow's citizens to make it worse.

78.

Keep green plants in the classroom. They add beauty (as well as oxygen) and make the learning space seem less institutional.

79.

When you have to give a failing grade, try to make it clear that the *work* is unsatisfactory, not the student.

80.

You can't prepare students for an essay-test world with a fill-in-the-blanks curriculum. Think about it!

81.

Try to handle each student paper only once. "Working smarter" will keep you from second-guessing yourself and will save you time in the long run.

82.

Teach your students that one way to get the right answers is to ask the right questions. There's no such thing as a stupid question—as long as it reflects a sincere desire to learn.

83.

Take a tip from special education. Try to have an informal Individual Education Plan (IEP) in mind for every student. No student deserves less.

84.

Conduct a vision audit of your classroom. Check sight lines, glare, and blind spots. An obstructed view creates frustration and distraction.

85.

When the weather is too nice to stay inside, don't. A little fresh air and sunshine never hurt any lesson.

86.

Don't worry about defending or explaining what you do. Good teaching speaks for itself.

87.

Keep an instant camera in your classroom. There are always plenty of things to photograph and post, keep, or send home.

88.

The secret to good teaching is timing. You have to catch the student somewhere between "I can't believe I don't know this" and "It doesn't matter anymore."

89.

Give students continuous feedback. No poor grade should ever come as a surprise.

90.

Turn nonteaching chores into real-world learning experiences. Assign a student to take roll and learn how to compute percentage of attendance at the same time. Put students in charge of the class fund-raiser and teach them to "keep the books." Not all lessons have to come from textbooks.

91.

Use the news! Whatever subject or grade you teach, incorporate current events into your daily lessons. Not only do you get students in the habit of keeping informed, but also you connect your classroom to the real world.

92.

For those students who are reluctant to give oral reports, try a historical wax museum project. Have each pupil select and research a historic figure, prepare a brief report, dress in costume, and recite whenever someone presses his or her "start button." It seems like a game, but it's really good practice in giving an oral presentation. No one ever said that teachers can't be sneaky.

93.

When planning your lessons, don't always save the best for last. You may run out of time.

94.

Make it a point to keep mentioning good new books for students to read. Your testimonials can tweak their interest. You'll never know how many lifelong readers you get started this way.

95.

American students are not very good at geography, primarily because no one teaches it to them. Incorporate geographical information in your everyday lessons. Show students where things happen, where things come from, and where other people(s) live. It helps students understand their own place in the world.

96.

Don't rule out memorization. It's still a valuable teaching tool. What's worth remembering is worth memorizing.

97.

Don't waste too much time on spelling bees. Why give the most practice to those who need it least?

98.

Pay attention to climate control in the classroom. Temperature, humidity, and ventilation affect student performance. Part of good teaching is providing a "comfort zone" for learning.

99.

It's OK to use informal "slanguage" now and then, but be sure to use proper English and an adult vocabulary sometimes, too. Students must learn that there is different speech, just as there are different wardrobes, for different settings and occasions.

100.

Be as well-read and informed as possible, so you can spot plagiarism and/or "invented" information. Students need to learn that school isn't a scam and that they can't forge their way into the future.

101.

Use lots of stickers and stamps on student papers. They are shorthand for "I like your work."

102.

Don't let the first class after lunch be a lesson in lethargy. Spark things up with some "deskersizes" before starting the afternoon's work.

103.

Support alternative education. There are always students who need something different. No one approach fits all. Not even yours!

104.

Don't be distracted by decorative artwork on student papers. Look for substance behind the glitz. Sometimes the best work comes in modest packages. Remember the story of Lincoln writing the Gettysburg address on the back of an envelope?

105.

Kids love to beat their own record. Timing performances and charting progress are mighty motivators. When students compete against themselves, they always come in first.

106.

Along with Band-Aids, keep some spot remover and a sewing kit handy. Kids can't concentrate when they're worried about a stain, a missing button, or a torn shirt. Sometimes, kids' clothes need first aid too.

107.

Keep a duplicate set of textbooks at home, so you won't have to lug around a heavy backpack. There's nothing in your contract that says you have to be a beast of burden.

108.

Never teach the same lesson exactly the same way twice. There's always something you can improve or adapt to new circumstances.

109.

Interrupt what you're doing to point out a rainbow. Kids need to learn what you have to teach, but many need a few rainbows in their lives just as much.

110.

Check the acoustics in your classroom. Eliminate sound barriers and unnecessary background noise. (Research shows that one-third of today's students often miss up to 30 percent of all verbal communications in schools.) A sound education depends on being able to hear the teacher.

111.

Don't mistake teaching faster for teaching better. There's a natural pace to learning. Speeding up often confuses students.

112.

Stop giving extra-credit assignments; have students submit their own project proposals instead. Preparing a sound proposal can be the most important part of the learning process.

113.

Don't expect quantum leaps in student performance. Success is usually incremental. Learning, like baseball, is a game of inches.

114.

Hit television shows can be popular in the classroom as well. *Jeopardy* and *Wheel of Fortune* work well with all ages as vehicles for review. Who says learning can't be fun?

115.

Don't always seat students alphabetically or line them up by height. Think of the kids who are consistently put at the back of the room or at the end of the line. Everyone deserves to be first sometime.

116.

Take fire drills seriously. They're more than bothersome interruptions. Think of all the passengers on the *Titanic* who wished they'd paid closer attention during the lifeboat drill.

117.

When helping older students improve their writing, pass on these tips from professional editors:

- Don't start sentences with *There are.*

- Begin sentences in different ways and vary sentence length.

- Limit sentences to seventeen words or fewer.

118.

Occasionally, take a page from real life by using evaluation indicators that students readily recognize such as "two thumbs up," "three out of five stars," or "7 on a scale of 1-10." After all, the purpose of feedback is communication.

119.

Just as libraries have amnesty periods for overdue books, set aside a window of time when students can hand in late assignments without penalty. In learning, late is better than never.

120.

Winter seems like forever. Kids get "cabin fever" too. Save some of your best lessons, field trips, and surprises for that long stretch from December to March.

121.

Welcome standardized tests and national assessments. They help us focus. In the words of Tom Peters, "What gets measured, gets done."

122.

Be open to visiting teachers from other species. Sometimes a fly on the wall or an ant colony on the playground can teach lessons more important than the ones you had planned for the day.

123.

Conduct a debriefing session with your students after each unit. What went well? What didn't? What can make that unit better for future students?

124.

Have your students bury a time capsule containing popular school items of the day. It's a gift of history that today's students can give to tomorrow's learners.

125.

Problem-solving ability is mostly a matter of attitude. Teach students that problems are friends. Without them, there would be no challenge, no learning, and no victory.

126.

Experts in school reform suggest that lessons for twenty-first-century learners should be (1) student-centered, (2) discussion-oriented, and (3) focused on complex academic tasks. How do your lessons measure up?

127.

If the school board wants you to follow a strategic plan for your classroom, don't get uptight. Just write down your expectations for your students and yourself. Then, meet those expectations. It's that simple.

128.

Send a welcome-back postcard to each student the week before school starts. It's an easy way to get kids "hyped-up" about the new school year.

129.

Stress the importance of preparation. An unprepared student is just a failure waiting to happen.

130.

Incorporate a "Mission Impossible" theme into your lessons. Place enrichment exercises on audiocassette tapes introduced by the familiar, "Your mission, should you choose to accept it, is. . . ." Good teachers aren't above using gimmicks.

131.

Minimize transition time. Teach students to settle down quickly, to start work promptly, and to wrap up without dawdling. It's a way to lengthen the school day without changing the starting or ending times.

132.

Videotape a series of supplemental lessons for use by substitute teachers. The tapes will help preserve your presence in the classroom and make things run more smoothly in your absence.

133.

Looking for ways to facilitate classroom change? Here's what author Thomas L. Quick suggests: "Allow for some chaos in your order." "Upgrade permanent to temporary."

134.

Use cartoons to teach the proper use of quotation marks. Even young students can learn that the words inside a speech balloon in a cartoon or comic book should be inside quotation marks in written work.

135.

Don't cry over spilled milk (or paint or ink). Spills are a natural by-product of a busy classroom. When accidents happen, clean up quickly and try to minimize student guilt or embarrassment. You can even make mopping up something fun you do together.

136.

Take a tip from people who stock grocery shelves. Place the best references at eye level where kids will see them and pick them up first. Place less frequently used resources on higher or lower bookshelves.

137.

Sometimes let your students write the test items. You'll probably end up with tougher questions and fewer complaints about them.

138.

Is your list of basic school supplies up-to-date? Paper, pencils, paste, crayons, and scissors aren't enough anymore. Some schools now require computer disks and videotapes as well.

139.

In many of their hit songs, the Beatles referred to actual places where they had once lived in Liverpool. Use examples from popular songs to show students the importance of writing about the things they know firsthand. Who says that rock and roll can't be educational?

140.

Use games, contests, and puzzles to help teach difficult material. Kids don't know a topic is hard when they're having fun.

141.

Turn data-gathering into a scavenger hunt for information. The first student to find all the facts on the list wins. There's no reason that the "grunt work" of learning has to be boring.

142.

Include students on curriculum committees. Listening to your "customers" is never a bad idea.

143.

If you're having difficulty getting students to write, try holding a "Liar's Contest" instead of giving a creative writing assignment. You'll be surprised how quickly students' interest perks up.

144.

Urge your principal to replace "daily announcements" with a student newscast. The students involved will learn valuable presentation skills, and other students will be more attentive. Scenic Heights Elementary School in Minnetonka, Minnesota, telecasts its morning "news" to all classrooms over channel KRTS (Kids Run This Station)!

145.

Whatever you teach, include some career information. You never know when unsuspecting students will stumble across their life's work.

146.

Looking for a classroom pet? Consider the funny, furry ferret. Kids love them. Teachers do, too, because ferrets instinctively seek out corners when they go to the bathroom. Just spread papers in all the corners. Voilà! Easy cleanup.

2.

Student Relations

147 Don't be conned by kids. Never believe everything students tell you about what other teachers do or allow in their classrooms.

148.

Be silly with your students sometimes. They need to know you're human too.

149.

Treat all students alike—fairly! There are no favorites in a master teacher's classroom.

150.

Be a cheerleader for all your students. Cheer loudest for the children who have the fewest fans in their corner.

151.

Dare to touch the kids. They need it more than ever before. Hugging a child who needs it isn't sexual harassment. It's caring. And that's what good teaching is all about. (Note: To avoid any possible misunderstandings, always follow your school's guidelines regarding touching students.)

152.

Pay attention to the culture of your classroom. Don't let it just happen. Create an atmosphere in which every child feels welcomed and wanted. The medium is part of the message.

153.

Don't tell students they have failed without also telling them where they can go for help and how they can still reach their goals. Good teachers never leave students stuck at a dead end.

154.

Help students make healthy choices by teaching them to ask, "Does this fit with who I am?"

155.

Downplay appearance. Help female students, especially, celebrate their individual talents and interests and establish their identity based on qualities other than appearance, popularity, or sexuality.

156.

Keep your word. If students can't trust their teacher, whom can they trust?

157.

Use the power of self-disclosure. If you open up to students, they will open up to you.

158.

Don't feel that you have to be everybody's buddy. Your students already have friends. What they need is a teacher.

159.

Be sure your students know where you stand on important issues such as drugs, gangs, and violence. Students look to you for guidance. Give them some.

160.

Let your faith in teaching and learning guide your actions. Show your students that you believe all kids can learn. There are no throwaway kids in a master teacher's classroom.

161.

Avoid labeling children. Kids tend to live down to the labels adults give them.

162.

Expect the best. You'll probably get it. Teacher expectations often become self-fulfilling prophecies. Children (and adults) tend to live up to the success others predict for them.

163.

Let your students know that you won't back off or go away. When they find out that you won't give up on them or on yourself, they won't either.

164.

Anticipate that students will search out and try to exploit your weaknesses. It's what they do best. Don't worry. You can handle it. You're the grown-up in the crowd.

165.

Search out "home-alone" kids and set up a volunteer telephone network to check regularly on each child's welfare.

166.

Don't feel that you always must have the answer to every student's problem. There are times when the most you have to offer is a tissue. Sometimes that's enough.

167.

Allow your students to have a bad day now and then. Allow yourself to have one too.

168.

If you must choose between working with papers and working with kids, choose kids every time!

169.

Be consistent and avoid sending mixed messages. Students shouldn't have to guess which teacher is going to show up.

170.

Don't meddle in your students' lives, but don't let bad things happen to good kids without trying to help.

171.

Don't "futurize" by telling students, "You'll never amount to anything." The future isn't something you can predict. It's something you create.

172.

Support extracurricular activities. They are the allies, not the competitors, of the classroom. Many students are drawn by the activities and end up achieving in academics as well.

173.

Don't pick a "student of the week." Pick a group of pupils each week. That way, everybody can be included sometime during the year. It doesn't hurt anyone to be recognized. It does hurt to be left out!

174.

Don't patronize students. They may not know what to call it, but they'll know what you're doing and they'll hate it.

175.

Don't promise what you can't deliver. Raising false hopes isn't fair to students.

176.

Be careful what you write on a student's paper. Critical comments may hurt more than you intended.

177.

Never stifle or belittle a child's imagination. Good teachers are dream-makers, not dream-busters.

178.

Set your students up for success. (It may be a new experience for some of them.) Once students know what success feels like and what it takes to get it, they'll take it from there.

179.

Realize that critical-thinking skills aren't just for gifted students. All kids can learn how to think better.

180.

Never define any child by an IQ score. There are lots of different kinds of intelligence. They all count.

181.

Give students many choices. Making choices sharpens their teeth for biting off bigger decisions later on.

182.

Remember that "tough love" applies to teaching too. Sometimes doing what seems unfair or unreasonable is really in your students' best interests. Do what's right—even if it hurts for a little while.

183.

Build on strengths. Continually dwelling on weaknesses is discouraging for you and for your students.

184.

Don't lend or give students money for lunch. If necessary, buy them lunch tickets. That way, you're sure how the money has been spent.

185.

Teach students to trust and value their own instincts. If they're uncomfortable doing something, they need to have the self-confidence to say "no."

186.

Never tease students unless you know they can take it. What seems funny to an adult may be intimidating or embarrassing to a little child.

187.

Learn the student jargon du jour. Know what your kids are talking about. If you know their language, you'll understand your students more and embarrass yourself less.

188.

Be honest with students. If you always tell the truth, you don't have to try to remember your lies.

189.

Don't expect students to look up to you if you talk down to them.

190.

Never jump on a student's idea before it has a chance to fly.

191.

Don't be too quick to criticize what students read. Reading something is better than reading nothing.

192.

Keep giving your students signs that show you care (for example, thumbs-up, a nod, a wink, or a touch). You can't assume kids know how you feel. Caring about and respecting them are the qualities students want most in a teacher.

193.

The most precious gift you have to give is your time. Give some to each student every day.

194.

Enjoy your students. It's the only way to survive as a teacher. They will disappoint you sometimes. They may even break your heart at times. More often, they will surprise, amaze, and delight you. Those are the moments that make it all worthwhile.

195.

Learn to watch for the early signs of eating disorders—especially in female students. These are socially transmitted diseases. Our culture is the carrier. Teach students that the world isn't just about being thin.

196.

Eat lunch with your students now and then. You'll be surprised what you can learn from "dinner-table conversation" at school.

197.

Don't be put off by what you see. Keep in mind that no student smells bad or looks dirty on the inside.

198.

If a student brings you a problem you can't handle, don't handle it. Refer it to the appropriate specialists. Know your limits.

199.

Be realistic. When early adolescents have to choose between hormones and homework, hormones win almost every time. Don't give up. Try to keep students focused. Make assignments lively and interesting. Most of all, remain patient. Kids can learn in spite of puberty!

200.

Be your best when your students are at their worst! Show sensitivity in times of special needs such as a job loss, divorce, physical or sexual abuse, loss of a loved one (including pets), or drug problems in the home.

201.

Everyone needs leadership training. Don't always pick the same kids.

202.

Don't look down on kids with tattoos or pierced skin. Fashion is neither good nor bad. Beauty and "cool" are in the eye of the beholder.

203.

Never walk away from a child who has no place to go.

204.

Accept that your students can have ideas that are as good or better than yours. Do it their way sometimes.

205.

Treasure any gift a student gives you no matter how inexpensive. The true value is in the giving, not in the gift.

206.

Help your students to see that it isn't just the disabled student who benefits from inclusion. All students benefit. Teachers do too.

207.

Join your students in regular visits to a homebound classmate who has a long-term illness. It's scary to feel separated and isolated as a young person. Help the student continue to feel a part of your class.

208.

Respect what ethnic groups want to be called (for example, African American, Latino or Hispanic, or Native American).

209.

Take time to visit with former students. They can tell you what you did right.

210.

Let your students see you studying, reading, and working hard. Your everyday example is a powerful teaching tool.

211.

Ask students for their opinions—
often! Kids are often told; they are
seldom asked. They'll feel good that
you cared what they think, and you'll
pick up some valuable insights and
ideas in the process.

212.

Be an ombudsman for ornery kids.
Orneriness can simply be another
form of creativity. Think of how
many brilliant and successful adults
were once troublemakers in school.

213.

You don't have to love every student,
but they don't know that. Let it be
your secret.

214.

When tragedy strikes your school (for example, the death of a student or faculty member), don't act as though it's business as usual. It isn't. Allow pupils to talk about their feelings. Permit grieving. It's a natural reaction.

215.

Startle your students with your peripheral vision. (It can be improved through practice and exercise.) Classroom management is easier when students think you have "eyes in the back of your head."

216.

If you're afraid of bugs, don't show it. Students love to torment teachers about their fears.

217.

When former students thank you for what you did for them, thank them in return for all they did for you!

218.

Don't always feel you have to make a point or teach a lesson every minute of the day. Sometimes a little friendly conversation with a caring adult is what some students need most.

219.

Strive to remember last year's students so you can call them by name. By doing this, you model respect for others. It's one way to continue to teach a valuable lesson even after students leave your classroom.

220.

Pay attention to the weather. It has an impact on learning. Dramatic weather shifts, extreme temperatures, high humidity, and prolonged dreariness— all can affect students' concentration. Good teachers adjust for weather conditions.

221.

Let students with Attention Deficit Disorder (ADD) know that they aren't crazy or stupid. They just process things differently. Life with ADD is a little harder, but it's definitely more interesting!

222.

Don't spend much time fault-finding. Blaming is looking backward. Solutions require moving forward.

223.

When you see students who are "natural teachers," encourage them. It's never too early to start recruiting tomorrow's miracle workers.

224.

Don't merely respond to what students ask. Answer the questions they may be afraid to ask, because they don't want to be embarrassed or look dumb. Good teachers need a touch of ESP. It comes with experience.

225.

Never think of students as "the enemy." It's your job to fight for them, not with them.

226.

As a teacher, you have countless decisions to make, but only one standard to apply: what is best for the kids?

227.

If you want to learn another language in order to communicate better with students, consider "signing." After all, your foreign students will eventually learn English. Your hearing-impaired students probably will never learn to hear.

228.

If you don't expect students to be perfect, they will never disappoint you.

229.

Mix the cliques. Don't allow the same self-selected cliques to work together all the time. Rearrange groups so that all pupils experience diversity.

230.

Lice aren't leprosy, but they are infectious nuisances that spread faster than rumors. Report any signs of lice to the "intensive hair unit" in your school nurse's office.

231.

Businesses use exit interviews. Why not schools? When students leave your class in mid-year, ask them what worked, what didn't, and why.

232.

Watch for the child who's having a bad day. You can turn it around. Smile. Say or do something nice. You can be a day-brightener for any child.

233.

Don't interrupt or finish sentences for students who stutter. Let them complete their thought. Stuttering is often a temporary phase in very young children. Patience is a big part of good teaching.

234.

It's OK for kids to have a crush on their teacher. It's not OK for teachers to encourage it. Always make it clear that you're the teacher—nothing more, nothing less!

235.

Avoid comparing siblings. No child should have to start out being "second best" or found "guilty by bloodline."

236.

Have a short memory for mistakes, failures, and behavior slips. Every child deserves a fresh start each morning.

237.

On a good day, your students will surprise you. On a bad day, your students will surprise you. Don't be surprised by surprises.

238.

No matter how long you teach, don't think you've seen it all. There isn't any "all." Students come in infinite varieties.

239.

Never refuse to give individual help when asked. Find the time. Find the energy. Find a way. Anything less is unacceptable.

240.

Don't underestimate your students' maturity. Let them make decisions commensurate with their comfort level. Teachers are supposed to stretch students, not constrict them.

241.

If you have occasion to buy a present for a student, give a learning gift. Books and magazine subscriptions always make good gifts from teachers.

242.

If students hang around your classroom before and after school, they must want to talk. Make it easy. Break the ice. Reach out before they lose their nerve and you lose an opportunity to teach or help.

243.

Recognize and reward all learners—not just the aggressive and assertive students. Quiet children also deserve their time in the sun.

244.

Telling bad jokes is common to students of all ages. Laugh at their childish attempts at humor. After all, they laugh at yours.

3.

Student Discipline and Classroom Management

245 Structure the classroom space so you can move around and get close to every student. (Try a U-shape arrangement.) Be everywhere in your classroom.

246.

Allow some constructive noise in the classroom. Noise can actually help settle down restless students. Dr. Harlen Hansen, of the University of Minnesota, states: "Good noise means learning. Bad noise means the children are out of control. No noise means adults don't understand the nature of children."

247.

Reserve a "limbo seat" in the classroom for any student who can't function or focus in his or her regular seat for the day.

248.

Establish a student grievance procedure in your classroom, and hold periodic "sound-off" sessions so students can vent frustrations and identify problems.

249.

Don't be a historian. Avoid prejudging students on the basis of past experiences or family history.

250.

Seek feedback. Evaluate yourself as well. Be tough. You can't get better if you don't know how you're doing. If report cards are good for kids, they should be good for teachers too!

251.

Put safety first. Make your classroom a safe haven for every child. Insist on zero tolerance for fighting, bullying, or harassment. If kids don't feel safe, they can't learn.

252.

Practice amnesty. The best teachers give lots of second chances and don't bear grudges.

253.

Teach conflict resolution skills—active listening, positive body language, brainstorming solutions, reflecting feelings, problem-solving, and others—as an alternative to violence. Kids need to learn how to settle disputes peacefully both in and out of the classroom.

254.

Always present classroom rules with conviction. Avoid any hint of questioning, uncertainty, pleading, or negotiating. If students think there's some wiggle room, they'll wiggle. Take your rules seriously, and your students will too.

255.

Discipline Tip: When problems occur, have the students involved call their parents in your presence to report the trouble, rather than calling yourself. You'll be surprised what a difference it makes when everybody hears the same story.

256.

Try not to "lose it" no matter how much you're tested. If students see they've angered you, they know they've beaten you at the discipline game.

257.

Keep reminding yourself that the most unpleasant student you have is probably the one who needs you most.

258.

Use a variety of positive reinforcers, such as free computer time, being first in line, or time to sit with a friend, to motivate students. "Whatever works" is always the best choice.

259.

Get by with as few rules as possible. Make 'em simple and make 'em stick.

260.

Don't waste time walking on eggs or soft-pedaling consequences. Say what has to be said and move on.

261.

Avoid sarcasm. It seldom helps and often hurts—a lot!

262.

Never punish children because you don't like their parents. Kids are not responsible for how their parents behave.

263.

Document all your disciplinary actions. Notes and records are important in today's litigious society. A good paper trail can lead you out of a lawsuit.

264.

Know what works in disciplining students. The tools of effective classroom management for the twenty-first century include the following:

- Empowering
- Facilitating
- Modeling
- Cheerleading
- Resourcing
- Advocating
- Coaching
- Mentoring
- Influencing
- Negotiating

265.

Enforce zero tolerance for racial or sexist slurs. Let your classroom be a model for what life should be like everywhere.

266.

Avoid practicing entrapment. Don't tempt kids to cheat. Leaving the room while a test is in progress is not a good idea.

267.

Never look the other way when you suspect physical or sexual abuse. A child's security may be a matter of life and death.

268.

Don't punish students when you're angry or grade papers when you're too tired. Your students deserve you at your best.

269.

Learn the signs of gang presence and report them when you spot them in your school or community. Gangs are only as strong as the community allows them to become.

270.

Know who has made you angry. If you are angry with yourself or your spouse, don't vent your anger on your students.

271.

Pay attention to attendance. If a student misses your class too often, find out why.

272.

Be aware of what's going on around you. Schools aren't always safe places to be—especially after school hours and after dark.

273.

Don't nag or plead with students. If they don't respond after two requests, take appropriate action.

274.

Remember that due process is for everyone. All students have a right to advance notice, a full hearing, and access to appeal.

275.

Model precaution. It's an important survival skill. Always lock up valuables. Unattended classrooms are easy targets for amateur (and professional) thieves.

276.

Use individual contracts with students and parents to spell out discipline expectations and consequences. People respect contracts. There's power in a document you have to sign.

277.

Take any student suicide threat seriously. You can't afford not to. Get help immediately.

278.

Be careful what you write down about students and keep in your files. Don't assume that your personal notes are private. The power of the subpoena is far-reaching today.

279.

When you feel overwhelmed, take your teaching one day at a time. If you deal successfully with today, you will always be ready for tomorrow.

280.

Watch for signs of sexual harassment in the classroom. If in doubt, apply this three-step test:

- Would you want your child treating others this way?

- Would you want a member of your family treated this way?

- Would the behavior be offensive if it were videotaped and viewed by people you respect and trust?

281.

If you suspect students are cheating on tests, reverse the order of the questions or use different forms for different individuals or groups. Don't tempt fate (or weak students).

282.

Don't be naive. Some kids today are ruthless and remorseless. They pose a real threat. Don't think you're invincible or assume that you can work wonders with everyone. Some students are more than you can handle. They need special help. Be alert. Know your limits. Don't do anything stupid that may put you or your pupils in danger.

283.

Whenever students line up, always stand at the back of the line. It's better to see what's going on ahead of you, than to trust what's happening behind you.

284.

Control your anger. The following seven steps of anger management have helped many teachers and can work for you too:

- 🍎 Understand what angers you.

- 🍎 Know your limits (tolerance level).

- 🍎 Know the symptoms of your anger.

- 🍎 Avoid anger-producing situations.

- 🍎 Say what's bothering you.

- 🍎 Do something physical.

- 🍎 Act out your anger in positive ways.

285.

Use stories, open-ended questions, and personal example to teach basic responsibilities. They work better than preaching for most pupils.

286.

Report all suspicious-looking packages or objects. "Good things" may come in small packages, but so do bombs.

287.

You know you're a good teacher when your students do what they're supposed to do, even when you're not looking.

288.

Teach kids that reporting drugs or weapons in school isn't snitching—it's survival!

289.

If you're worried about concealed weapons in school, suggest requiring "see-through" backpacks. They are already working in many schools.

290.

Start and end each day with some comfortable rituals. Kids need anchors to stay focused and to reduce internal stress.

291.

Never try to shout over a noisy classroom. Talk "under the noise" instead. Factory workers first learned this trick on the assembly line in World War II.

292.

Your responsibility doesn't end at your classroom door. If you spot trouble anywhere in the school, it's not someone else's problem. It's yours.

293.

Don't get into a shouting match with students. You can't win, and you may lose your dignity and respect in the process.

294.

Dare to be a teacher who tests everything. If it's important, it's worth measuring. If it's unimportant, you shouldn't be teaching it anyway.

295.

Don't give students your home E-mail address unless you're open to anonymous insults, obscenities, and other assorted "cyber garbage."

296.

Be diligent in enforcing your school's discipline plan, but give all students a clean slate periodically—maybe once each quarter.

297.

Don't penalize children for being children. Wiggling and asking "Why?" are natural behaviors, not misbehaviors.

4.

Working with Parents, Colleagues, and the Community

298 Don't be too proud to scrounge for free stuff. You can't have too many resources for learning, and your classroom budget will never be big enough.

299.

Match up every student with a caring adult in the school or the community. Enlist custodians, secretaries, aides, and other staff members if necessary. It's important that all children have some grown-up they can go to with questions and concerns.

300.

Help other teachers (particularly beginners). It's not like you're movie stars competing for the same roles. There are plenty of kids to go around for everyone.

301.

Always use plain talk with parents. They need help and direction, not mumbo jumbo. Using big words and jargon won't make you a better teacher. Communicating clearly will.

302.

Don't forget about grandparents. Include and involve them in intergenerational school activities whenever possible. Grandparents make great aides, mentors, readers, storytellers, and listeners. They also bring a special patience, love, and wisdom into the classroom. What child couldn't use an extra grandma or grandpa?

303.

Make home visits. Good teachers don't hide in the school. If your students live in a rough neighborhood, take along a friend or ask a counselor or social worker to join you. If you can't visit every family, at least visit the homes of all newcomers and those students who are seriously falling behind.

304.

Start a "Catch-22" program in your classroom. Urge parents to "catch" twenty-two minutes of quality, one-on-one time with their child each day—reading, talking, or playing together. (Twenty-two minutes daily isn't much, but it's much more than the national average of thirty minutes a week.)

305.

Don't teach in a vacuum. Good teachers learn from each other. Network. Team teach. Find a way to connect with peers. Even professionals need a support group.

306.

Welcome other adults into your classroom for four reasons:

- It's the best possible public relations policy.

- All students love an audience.

- Guests make the classroom seem more like part of the real world.

- You have nothing to hide.

307.

Don't be too hard on parents. They send you their very best, and most work hard at raising their kids. And they don't get summers off.

308.

Take time to serve as a broker of social services. See to it that your students' families get whatever kind of help they need. It's not in the job description, but it's part of the teaching life.

309.

Use native speakers and interpreters to inform and involve non-English-speaking parents.

310.

Network worldwide. There's no reason for any teacher to feel isolated anymore. Use E-mail and the Internet to exchange ideas with other teachers around the globe.

311.

Insist that transportation and child care services be provided for all school functions. Serving a light meal is a good idea, too. Removing obstacles for parents is the school's part of the bargain.

312.

Lobby for a Family Resource Center in your school where families can check out videos, software, educational toys and games, and self-help books on parenting. If parents are going to be lifelong learners, the school must become a lifelong resource for learners.

313.

Involve all students in community service learning projects. In the words of Marian Wright Edelman, "Service is the rent we pay for living."

314.

Seek out a local business to adopt your classroom. This association will be good for your students and for the business as well.

315.

Facilitate discussions in which parents can agree on guidelines for television viewing, computer use, alcohol-free parties, and working hours for minors. A uniform front is the parents' best defense against student at-risk behaviors.

316.

Encourage parents and students to sign a covenant to support learning and to work for better schools. People try harder when they're "under contract."

317.

Respect what parents know about their own children. Teachers don't always know best.

318.

Keep an up-to-date list of competent tutors to give to students or parents who need them. You can't help everyone all by yourself.

319.

Distribute a simple weekly or monthly parent newsletter. Parents can't help you or their child if they don't know what's going on at school.

320.

Establish clear-cut homework, makeup, and extra-credit policies, and see that parents and students know what they are. It's unfair for anyone to be surprised by what counts and what doesn't.

321.

Coordinate your testing schedule with that of other teachers. There's no reason for students to have tests coming at them from all directions at the same time.

322.

Make friends with the school secretary and the building custodians. They can be your most important allies.

323.

Get your paperwork done on schedule. It doesn't take any more time to be on time, and it builds goodwill with people who count.

324.

Don't bad-mouth other teachers or the school administration in public. You're supposed to be on the same team.

325.

Don't take on other teachers' problems. You'll have enough of your own.

326.

Be shameless! Copy what the best teachers do, and don't feel guilty about it.

327.

Tell parents what you would want to know if their child were yours.

328.

Be sensitive about how much homework you assign. Remember that your students and their families have a life beyond schoolwork. Church, sports, scouts, fun, and family are important too.

329.

Take your share of "bad kids" and "dirty duty" (such as lunchroom supervision or bus loading). They are part of being a real pro.

330.

Don't expect your principal or your union to bail you out when you do something unethical, unprofessional, or harmful to kids. When you cross that line, you're on your own.

331.

Don't ask others why they became a teacher. Some people come to teaching for the long summer vacations and stay for the long haul.

332.

Remind your colleagues that schools shouldn't be run for the convenience of adults.

333.

Practice good voice-mail etiquette. Check messages frequently and respond promptly. Good manners work just as well when recorded as they do in person.

334.

Include noncustodial parents in all mailings and classroom communications. The child is theirs too.

335.

Develop special "Parent Kits" to help families support their child's learning. Include homework hints, summer activity ideas, and tips on good books for kids.

336.

Urge your principal to have all parent letters translated into the appropriate language(s) for immigrant families. Strangers in a strange land need all the help they can get. It might as well start with the school.

337.

Teach your students to treat substitute teachers as guests in the classroom. (You want them to feel welcome, so they'll accept your invitation to return when you need them.) Assign one student to introduce the "guest" to the class in your absence and to review your daily routine for the substitute.

338.

Have your students conduct their own parent-teacher conferences sometimes. It will "wow" the parents and make the kids more accountable.

339.

Seek out positive minority male and female mentors. They're not always easy to find, but they're desperately needed.

340.

Make a big fuss over volunteers, aides, and substitutes. You couldn't do business without them.

341.

If parents don't want you to call them with problems, do it anyway. Don't let parents off the hook by default. They have to be accountable, too.

342.

Avoid using negative labels (such as "broken home") when referring to single-parent families. There are numerous mended, blended, and extended families today, and they all can work!

343.

Try holding a difficult parent conference in a neutral setting. How about meeting for coffee at a nearby fast-food restaurant?

344.

Don't be afraid to show off what your students have learned. The media never hesitate to exploit school failures. Schools should publicize their successes!

345.

Encourage parents to adopt a bus stop. Things go better when adults monitor the loading and unloading of school buses. A good day at school begins and ends with a safe bus stop!

346.

Have your students call parents, senior citizens, and other special "guests" with invitations to classroom events. Who can turn down a child's invitation?

347.

Conduct your class in a local mall once a year. It's a great way for shoppers and community members to see the school in action.

348.

Hold coffee parties or brown-bag lunch sessions with parents. Informal contacts help build bridges between the home and the school.

349.

Never cover for an incompetent colleague. Supporting a coworker is one thing; enabling an unfit teacher to damage children is another. You have an obligation to all students, not just your own.

350.

Respect parents' pocketbooks. Limit requests for money. It's unfair to assume that all families can afford expensive field trips or special school supply items. Be sure that no children in your classroom are ever embarrassed because their families are on a strict budget.

351.

Lobby for a longer school year, but don't advocate taking summer completely away from children. Summertime is a special kind of education all by itself.

352.

With all the electronic wizardry at your command, don't forget one of the most versatile technologies of all—the telephone. Every classroom should have one. Use it often for up-close and personal contact with learning resources throughout the community and the world.

353.

Make a log of classroom disruptions (public-address announcements, pull-out programs, etc.) for a one-month period. Use the results to lobby your principal for more uninterrupted instructional time. Students don't learn best in fits and starts.

354.

Don't blame last year's teacher for this year's problems. There's no reward for finding fault. Work with what you have and do your best. Good teachers don't need excuses.

355.

If you share a classroom, respect the other teacher's privacy and property. Don't disturb your colleague's papers or use another's materials without asking. If little kindergartners can learn to share without arguing, grown-up teachers should be able to do the same.

356.

Pay attention to strangers in school. Introduce yourself; ask if you can help; direct them to the office; watch what they do and where they go; and notice details about their appearance. In violent times, students in school can become prey for predators. Don't let it happen on your watch!

357.

Urge parents to stay involved in their child's life, even through high school. It's a myth that adolescents are supposed to separate from their families and that parents are supposed to let them go. Teenagers and their parents need each other as much as ever—maybe more!

358.

Videotape student reports and presentations, and send them home for Mom and Dad to enjoy. Videos bring your classroom into their living room. What better way to cement the home-school partnership!

359.

Let parents help, but don't become beholden to anyone. It lays you open to accusations of favoritism or conflict of interest.

360.

Listen to older teachers. They have wisdom and experience. Listen to younger teachers. They have exuberance and boldness. Listen most to yourself. You, alone, know what you want to do and what you can do.

361.

Recruit retired teachers to help children in your classroom. It will keep the retirees in touch. More important, it will make your students the beneficiaries of several lifetimes of successful teaching. What a gift!

362.

Some night, instead of giving homework, assign your students to spend the time with their parents. What family couldn't use the unexpected gift of an evening together?

363.

Ask your school to provide personalized business cards. They work for other professionals. Why not teachers?

364.

Be kind to your assistant principals. When you've had a bad day, think of theirs. They have to handle attendance, discipline, and all the other tough tasks no one wants. Cheer up. Your job could be worse.

365.

When attending professional conferences, set aside plenty of time for networking and informal contacts with colleagues. These are often the best sources of new ideas, inspiration, healing, and growth.

366.

Don't be jealous of colleagues. Celebrate their successes and find out how they did it.

367.

If you join a team-teaching project, be sure it's for the right reasons. The goal should be to help kids learn better, not just make your job easier.

368.

Support your principal. The boss isn't always right, but he or she is always the boss.

369.

Have your class(es) send "Good Neighbor Awards" or thank-you notes to area residents. People who live around schools put up with extraordinary distractions. Let the neighbors know they are appreciated.

370.

Encourage parents to have a secret code word that must be given by any other adult who picks up their child from school. Precaution is part of doing business as a family today.

371.

Don't sign up for committees unless you plan to actively participate. It's unfair to other members. More important, you won't get anything out of it unless you put something into it. Dead wood doesn't grow.

372.

Don't leave everything for the custodians to do. Sometimes you and your class should clean up your own mess. It can be an important part of the lesson.

373.

Don't blame your problems on the state legislature. Nothing government does (or doesn't do) will make *you* a better teacher.

374.

Don't expect parents to spearhead school reform. Most parents want things to be the way they were when they went to school.

375.

Make friends with a pediatrician. You never know when you might need expert advice on a student's health-related learning problem.

376.

Ask school officials to conduct periodic tests to determine any dangerous levels of radon or carbon monoxide in the classroom. While you have their attention and cooperation, you might also ask them to check for asbestos and lead-based paints. Not all threats to students can be seen or smelled.

377.

Don't be duped into dispensing medications to students (not even an aspirin). Leave pharmacy functions to the school nurse. There are reasons why nurses follow strict guidelines. One of them is called avoiding a lawsuit.

378.

Use a wristwatch alarm to keep parent conferences on schedule. (For every sixty seconds one parent runs over, another is robbed of a minute of entitled teacher time.)

379.

Support school uniforms. "Clothes wars" put pressures on kids and families, distract from learning, and generate snobbery in the classroom. Calvin Klein never helped anyone learn better.

380.

Always have a "wish list" ready for parents, local businesses, the PTA, or anyone else who asks, "What do you need?" Good things come to those who are ready to receive them.

5.

Personal Development and Motivation

381 Organize your day—every day! Learning shouldn't be a hit-or-miss affair.

382.

Be yourself. Kids can spot phonies. Being a good teacher isn't an act.

383.

Look your best. You'll feel better and teach better. Businesspeople "dress for success." Why not teachers? (You'll be amazed how many of your students notice your earrings or necktie every day.)

384.

Have at least one silly rule for students to test and protest. It makes it easier for them to accept the rest of your limits.

385.

Don't settle for sloppy or second best. Excellence is always in fashion. The "dumbing down" of America will happen only if we let it. Don't let it.

386.

Put off procrastinating. You can't teach students anything tomorrow. You can only teach them today.

387.

Listen to yourself. Are you nagging? Whining? If you don't like what you hear, do something about it.

388.

Don't act as though you're always in a hurry. All children deserve someone who has time for them.

389.

Associate with winners. Hang out with the best teachers in your building. Greatness rubs off. So does mediocrity. Avoid the whiners and complainers. You've got more important things to do.

390.

Be physically rested and mentally ready for each day. Students always have lots of energy. You should too.

391.

Keep up with the latest technologies. Learn from the kids if you have to. If you're not computer literate, you may already be irrelevant in today's classroom.

392.

Practice pacing and prioritizing. Save time in your workday for advising, planning, and professional growth. Teaching is many things. Not all of them occur in front of a classroom full of kids.

393.

Don't take yourself too seriously. You're not the most important person in the classroom.

394.

Do whatever it takes to stay fresh throughout the entire school day (for example, don't skip breaks; practice stretching exercises; take mini-mental vacations). The last lesson of the day deserves the same energy and enthusiasm as the first.

395.

Pay attention to complaints. They are another way to help you grow. Critics can be teachers too.

396.

Admit it when you don't know something, and never hesitate to ask for help when you need it. It's OK for teachers to have warts. Students are more comfortable learning from real-life human beings than from icons.

397.

Be aware of your body language. Sometimes your posture, gestures, or facial expressions speak louder than your words.

398.

Believe in miracles. They happen in your classroom every day!

399.

Get a life of your own outside of teaching. Both you and your students deserve it.

400.

Stay home when you're ill. That's what sick leave is for. Would you want some sick person teaching your child?

401.

Learn something new every day. Good teachers are good students first.

402.

Show that you like your job and your students. Your attitude provides the energy that drives the classroom.

403.

Talk less. Listen more. A big part of teaching is learning from your students.

404.

When your plate is full, don't take seconds. Learn to say "No." It's a survival skill for busy teachers.

405.

Trust your instincts. If a course of action doesn't feel right, back off for awhile.

406.

Save some time for reflection each day. Examine what you're doing and why. Have a plan. You want your teaching to be more than a series of knee-jerk reactions.

407.

Accept failure—your students' and your own. Learn from it and move on. As Zig Zigler says, "Failure is an event, not a person."

408.

Remember why you became a teacher to renew your commitment. The old reasons (love of kids, interest in helping others, and a desire to make a difference) still make sense.

409.

Don't feel that you always have to go back to school every summer to improve as a teacher. Sometimes doing something different (or doing nothing) can make you a better teacher.

410.

Remember, it's a teacher's job to make things better, but if you can't fix certain things, at least don't make them worse.

411.

Dare to show a little "raw patriotism" once in awhile. With so many cynics around, someone has to remind our children that our country is still worth getting emotional about.

412.

Be a model of civility. Kids don't see enough of it in our society.

413.

Most kids start out loving school. Many end up hating it. What do teachers do to take the joy out of learning in the interim? Think about it!

414.

Rehearse your lessons. It's not just students who need practice.

415.

Remember what it was like to be a student. This perspective will change the way you teach.

416.

Never say, "I'm just a teacher." What you do is powerful and important. Too many teachers are victims of their own self-deprecation. If you don't respect your profession, who will?

417.

If your students are confused, ask yourself, "Who's confusing them?"

418.

Don't take work home every night. Your students shouldn't have homework seven nights a week and neither should you.

419.

Don't act childish when things don't go right. There's supposed to be an adult in every classroom. It's you!

420.

Recall all the dumb things your teachers did when you were in school—and don't do them.

421.

Ask yourself, "If school isn't fun, whose fault is it?"

422.

All teachers make mistakes. Good teachers admit them. Be one of the good ones.

423.

Look in the mirror and like what you see. You have to feel good about yourself before you can build your students' self-esteem.

424.

Remember that you don't have to be smarter than your students. You don't even have to be bigger than your students. But you should be more mature than your students.

425.

Pray for your students and for yourself. You both need all the help you can get. You may not be able to do it at school, but you can always pray at home.

426.

Realize that master teaching is always a work in progress. Times change. Students change. Teachers must change too. ("You can never step into the same river twice.") If you teach tomorrow like you teach today, you should have quit teaching yesterday!

427.

Dare to be different. Every teacher should have a unique "batting stance" in the classroom.

428.

Remember that the first step to successful teaching is to "show up!" Take your own attendance as seriously as you do your students'.

429.

Adopt this teacher's creed: "Don't blame. Don't shame. And let everyone play the game."

430.

Voluntarily change assignments periodically. Try a new subject, grade level, or school. People, like plants, grow better if they're repotted from time to time.

431.

Respond to setbacks with renewed effort. Giving up is not an effective teaching technique.

432.

Stress lifelong learning. Not everyone goes on to college, but life doesn't run out of lessons for any of us.

433.

Face your own prejudices. Be aware of how you treat people who are different.

434.

Remember that just because kids today are seeing more, hearing more, doing more, questioning more, and ignoring us more, doesn't mean they need us less.

435.

Don't rely on others for approval or validation. You know when you've done the right thing, and your students know when you've helped them. That should be enough.

436.

Remember that anything that makes you a better person makes you a better teacher too.

437.

Make good manners the way you do business in your classroom. It doesn't take any more time to be polite, and it makes working together a lot more pleasant.

438.

Think about the teachers who inspired you most. You can't be them, but you can find ways to be more like them.

439.

Be one of the best teachers who are still teaching their best on the last day of school.

440.

Work on your weaknesses. Keep trying to do better and to be better. Don't let a mediocre career just happen.

441.

Pay attention to your posture. Good posture keeps you fresh, boosts your confidence, and makes you look more like the teacher.

442.

If you take credit for your students' successes, be willing to accept some blame when they fall short.

443.

Don't be defined by your college major or limited by what it says on your teaching license. A good English teacher can teach a lot about health, and a good health teacher can teach a lot about English.

444.

Watch students entering and leaving your classroom. Their faces will tell you a lot about your teaching.

445.

Never give up hope. No good teacher can be a good pessimist.

446.

Show pride in your school. Wear the school colors. Know the school song. Pride is infectious. Unlike most infections, however, pride makes individuals and organizations perform better.

447.

It's OK for teachers to get dirty in the line of duty. Don't worry about your appearance if you get mussed up or messed up helping children. God will forgive you—and so will the kids.

448.

Be a squeaky wheel. Your students deserve as much grease as anyone.

449.

Pay attention to your penmanship. It matters. If scribbling is the best you can do, why should your students try to do any better?

450.

Refuse to become cynical. If you feel cynicism coming on, visit a nursery for newborns. Attend a confirmation class or a bar mitzvah. Go to a high school graduation. Kids and magic still go together. Teachers are part of that. Who can be cynical?

451.

Recognize the power of handwritten notes. Computer printouts, faxes, and voice-mail messages are fine; but personal notes, handwritten by the sender, carry more clout. Use them often.

452.

Dare to videotape your teaching. See yourself as your students see you. Even the best teaching performance can improve with a little editing.

453.

If your teaching doesn't leave time for your own learning, try enrolling in the "Automobile University." There are many educational tapes that can improve your knowledge and skill while you drive.

454.

Remember that each class of students is like a farmer's annual crop. Some are better than others, but they all take the same loving care in order to get the highest yield.

455.

Don't be too upset by what students say about you. Be more upset if they never talk about you at all. That means you're not having an impact on their lives.

456.

Be persistent. The secret of successful teachers is that they may fail frequently, but they never quit.

457.

Never put union matters, school politics, or career advancement before the interests of students. Children come first—period!

458.

Remember that you don't have to try to be younger than you are in order to teach young children. They will accept you at any age if you will only act your age.

459.

Think about the things that irritate and frustrate you in the advanced college courses you take. Avoid making the same mistakes with your students. After all, you should learn something in graduate school.

460.

Remember the good times in the bad times. It helps you know that things will get better.

461.

Reread your childhood diary. It will remind you that relationships are sometimes more important than academics. That's why students aren't always as excited as you are about conjugating a verb or solving a math equation.

462.

Spend time with people who aren't teachers. If teachers talk only to other teachers, they begin to think that school and schooling are all that matter. They aren't. Kids know that. You should too.

463.

Take care of your feet. The secret of successful teaching is wearing comfortable shoes!

464.

Keep a little candy on hand. It can be a lifesaver for a diabetic child, a special treat for a student who deserves a reward, or a source of quick energy for a fading teacher.

465.

Did you ever wonder how all those outspoken critics of education got so smart if the schools are so bad? School-bashing isn't new. Don't take it personally. You know better than anyone else how good or how bad your school is.

466.

You don't have to be the best teacher in the school to be a success, but you have to be the best teacher you can be to avoid being a failure.

467.

Just because you're having a bad day doesn't mean that your students must have one as well. Get a grip! Make something good happen for every child every day—even on the bad days.

468.

When you're low, remember that in most households, you are the most important person in the world outside the family circle. In emergencies, a doctor or plumber may temporarily be more important, but usually, the teacher is the most significant person beyond the immediate family. Who says teaching isn't a prestigious profession?

469.

Don't wear too much perfume or cologne. Some students are allergic. Besides, you may attract bees in season.

470.

The good thing about teaching is that students are always watching you. The bad thing about teaching is that students are always watching you. If you don't like scrutiny, get out of teaching.

471.

If you think you can handle the truth, read Tracy Kidder's *Among School Children*. It will force you to understand what it's like on the other side of the desk.

472.

Even if your school isn't ranked at the top, your classroom can be tops. Don't catch mediocrity from those around you.

473.

Teaching can be easy. Good teaching never is. Work hard at what you do. Earn the title of "Teacher."

474.

"Use the past as a guide, not a leaning post" (Gordon Rausch, retired teacher).

475.

When you fall behind and more work is piling up, *refuse to panic*. Just do the next thing and then the next. Keep it up. Things will get better.

476.

Avoid the one cardinal sin all teachers fear committing—falling asleep in your own class!

477.

Keep fit. Your kids need you in top shape. As the prolific source of wisdom, "Anonymous," asks, "If you ruin your body, where will you live?"

478.

Remember that good teachers always plan to be spontaneous and are a lot better organized than they appear to be.

479.

"Near the end of the year, a teacher can't help facing the fact that there's a lot she hoped to do and hasn't done and now probably never will. It's like growing old, but for teachers old age arrives every year." (Tracy Kidder, *Among School Children*, 1989)

480.

To teach, stay teachable!

481.

Quit complaining about paperwork. Wherever there are teachers and students, there will be papers to grade. Get used to it.

482.

Don't be afraid of accountability. It's just a matter of promising only what you can deliver and delivering whatever you promise. You can do that.

483.

Just because you're not sure what you're doing doesn't mean that your kids have to know it. Sometimes bluffing is an essential survival skill for teachers.

484.

Guilt is destructive. Don't use it on students. Don't use it on parents. And don't use it on yourself.

485.

Don't become so specialized that you can't help students with the basics in other subjects. When a teacher claims ignorance of another teacher's subject, students wonder why they should learn it.

486.

If teaching is just a job to you, you're merely a technician, not a real teacher. The difference is passion!

487.

Learn about the history of your school. This knowledge will help you convey a sense of pride and tradition to your students.

488.

Every teacher should coach or advise an after-school activity. Seeing each other in different roles and settings helps you and your students accept each other as human beings.

489.

Good schools don't happen by accident. Teachers make them that way. Are you doing your share to make the whole school better?

490.

Don't be afraid of competition, such as parent vouchers to attend private schools. Good teachers will always attract good students.

491.

You may be teaching English or math or music, but you're also showing kids what being an adult is like. How you act is as important as how you teach.

492.

Curriculum, materials, methods, and relationships determine the conditions of learning. Of these four, relationships are the most important.

493.

Don't ask if you can afford to get more training. You can't afford not to. A good teacher never knows enough.

494.

Find a spot in the school where you can enjoy absolute silence for at least five minutes a day. Quietude is an elixir. A daily dose will help you feel better and teach better.

495.

Learn to write grant proposals. If you've got the ideas, someone else may have the money. Teachers get grants all the time. Why not you?

496.

If you don't get that transfer or special assignment you wanted, just make up your mind that it probably wasn't as good as it sounded anyway. Sour grapes are better than no grapes at all.

497.

Consider flu shots. Even the doctors on *ER* aren't exposed to as many germs as teachers are every day.

498.

Don't rush out the door too soon on the last day of school. Pause to think about the year. What worked? What didn't? What will you do differently? A little quiet reflection will bring closure to the term, free you up for the summer, and set you up for a running start in the fall.

499.

Sometime when you're working late and the building is quiet, listen to the voices of ghosts of teachers past. They'll all tell you, "It's worth it!"

500.

Know when to quit. If you start to lose your caring or enthusiasm, it's time to graduate from teaching. No child deserves a burned-out teacher.

501.

Thank God you're a teacher. It doesn't get any better than that!

About the
Author

Dr. Robert D. Ramsey is a lifelong educator and freelance writer from Minneapolis. His professional background includes front-line experience in three award-winning school districts in two different states as teacher, counselor, supervisor, curriculum director, adjunct professor, and associate superintendent.

Dr. Ramsey's previous publications include *Complete School Discipline Guide* (Prentice Hall) and

501 Ways to Boost Your Child's Self-Esteem (Contemporary Books). His popular writings have helped countless teachers to understand, instruct, and inspire today's children and youth. *501 Tips for Teachers* is yet another tool that teachers can use to be their best and do their best for all students—every day!